Hocus Pocus, you're Focused!

A Daydreamer's Guide to Developing Powers of Concentration

Arthur Laud

© 2012-2023

All Rights Reserved. No part of this publication may be reproduced in any form or by any means, including scanning, photocopying, or otherwise without prior written permission of the copyright holder.

Disclaimer and Terms of Use: The Author and Publisher have strived to be as accurate and complete as possible in the creation of this book, notwithstanding the fact that he does not warrant or represent at any time that the contents within are accurate due to the rapidly changing nature of the Internet. While all attempts have been made to verify information provided in this publication, the Author and Publisher assume no responsibility for errors, omissions, or contrary interpretation of the subject matter herein. Any perceived slights of specific persons, peoples, or organizations are unintentional. In practical advice books, like anything else in life, there are no guarantees of personal results. This book is not intended for use as a source of legal, business, accounting, medical, or financial advice. All readers are advised to seek services of competent professionals in the legal, business, accounting, medical, and finance fields. Furthermore, what works for some people may not work for others. Following the advice given in this book may result in unintended consequences in your life and the author and publisher assume no responsibility for that. Pursue the contents of this book at your own risk.

Table of Contents

Why you are So Easily Distracted 1

Why you Need Better Concentration 7

Getting in Touch with Your Reaction Reflexes 11

Rerouting Your "Distraction Circuit" into Concentration 15

Changing Your Daydreams into Productive Thinking 19

Learning NOT to Multitask 23

Five Ways to Conquer the Procrastination Habit . 27

Five Ways to Stop Forgetting Things 33

Focusing at Work 37

Focusing at Play 41

Focusing on Conversations 45

Meeting Deadlines 49

Five Fun Games that Help Develop Powers of Concentration 53

Conclusion 57

Why you are So Easily Distracted

Today's world is fast-paced and complex. We are all overloaded with tasks, and many of us face immense competition at work or school. With too much on our plates, it can become difficult to focus on the task at hand. When we lose focus we do a lousy job. So we trade off efficiency in the pursuit of productivity, without realizing that efficiency itself is a key ingredient to productivity. When you do a lousy job at something because of a lack of focus, oftentimes you are forced to do it again. It would have been more productive to have focused and done it right the first time.

In addition, some of us are natural daydreamers. We don't need any encouragement to become distracted – it happens naturally. All it takes is one interesting thought to side-track us off on some mental adventure and we miss everything that is happening in real time – even if it is our favorite subject!

Developing powers of concentration might seem to be a hopeless endeavor for a chronically busy person or a natural daydreamer, but it's really not that difficult. Learning to focus better can be accomplished through simple exercises that train your brain to stay on track. The first thing we want to do is to learn to recognize common factors which trigger our natural distraction. Each of us will have our own individual distraction triggers. They are nothing more than bad habits - and bad habits can gradually be replaced with good ones.

Personal Factors which Can Trigger Distraction

• Experiencing a troublesome relationship

• A hectic daily routine that always has you thinking 2-3 steps ahead

• Family concerns (such as an illness, or a child constantly getting into trouble)

• Ambition overload

• Excitement over a pending event (such as a coming vacation)

• Simply having a lot on your mind at the moment

Psychological Factors which Can Trigger Distraction

• Lack of confidence in your ability

• Friction in co-worker relationships

• Another project is always dominating your mind

• Being sad or even the beginnings of depression

• Memory problems

• Bored with your life

Physical Sources of Distraction

You could be distracted by something as simple as a falling leaf or fluttering butterfly if you are bored with your life or prone to daydreaming. Other potential sources of physical distractions include:

• Unproductive coworkers who socialize too much

• Your cell phone

• Social networking (Facebook, Twitter, etc.)

- Music (your favorite song comes on the radio)

- Gossip

- Instant messages

- Incoming email

- Addiction to a game (solitaire has destroyed companies)

- Noise of any kind, such as nearby construction or a distant TV

- Uninvited guests

Figuring Out What Can Be Changed

Hopefully some of those rang familiar bells. You should make a list at this point because it will be useful in the following chapters. Having identified the major sources of your usual distractions, we can now put up roadblocks to them, both physically and mentally. This will remove some of the stumbling blocks in your daily routine. The next step will be to figure out how to get you genuinely interested enough in the real world to want to stay there. In the meantime, here are a few quick tips to help you focus better

this very afternoon and feel better about yourself already:

- Decide to get something done. Pick a task, any task. A minor work thing or a personal errand.

- Discover ways to enjoy your work. If a project cannot be done single-handedly, indicate you preference to work in teams. If studying alone doesn't help, indulge in group studies or seek help from a tutor. Set deadlines for yourself and keep track of time to make the task more motivating and interesting.

- Get organized! Write down the requirements of a given task and the time period within which everything needs to be done. Start doing this for every important task. This routine will help you keep your mind straight and maintain consistency.

- Think about what you will achieve: You know successful completion of a task will result in some benefits and rewards. Consider the bonuses, over-time compensation, certification, scholarships etc. that you stand to gain. Keeping this in mind is a good way to motivate oneself and remain focused.

- Eat healthy for the rest of today. Nutritious food is what keeps your brain running. Doctors and researchers have linked a strong relationship between brain performance and a healthy diet. Make sure you have a well-balanced meal at least once per day (a good balance of low-fat protein and healthy carbohydrates). Eating right does wonders for keeping you active and engaged.

- Avoid stress, just for today. Research has shown that stress is a major contributor to reduced productivity. If you are stressed out about something, take a few deep breaths and consider taking a short walk and think yourself through it. Stress doesn't help. Stop worrying so much. Just get some stuff done and go home happy tonight.

Why you Need Better Concentration

Concentration is a natural ability that everyone has. Have you ever noticed children engaged in drawing or playing with their favorite toys? How about a sports-fanatic watching their favorite team play? You wouldn't be able to distract either of them, even if you danced around wearing a purple chicken suit shouting into a bullhorn. They are totally focused on what they are doing. From these examples you can see that concentration is not a difficult endeavor. We are all born the innate ability to focus when we want to. Anybody can do it. The trick is getting ourselves to *want to* focus on certain tasks that we are having trouble concentrating on.

If you tend to drift off during meetings and presentations, you will be at a disadvantage in your work environment because you will miss important bits of information that everybody else now has. You will need to waste time searching for it later. Ask your coworkers and they will probably reply, "You were at the meeting." This is not only embarrassing, it makes you seem unreliable and can keep you from getting promotions.

Does your spouse take too long to get to the point with their stories? Welcome to the club! My wife will include every little detail when telling me about something that happened at work, and drag the story out at a snail's pace. I guess women just like to talk or something. It is difficult to keep my attention that long when it seems that there is no point building. Something she says along the way will invariably trigger a thought process in my mind and I will go off who knows where while she keeps yacking. I catch myself earlier these days than I used to, but as you can imagine we have ended up in fights because of my drifting. I will pop back in at some point and then have to ask for details which were already given, and into the doghouse I go.

Work efficiency and domestic bliss are not the only reasons you should learn to stay focused. Being easily distracted is bad for your health. Traffic accidents often happen because a driver turned their head to look at something, became interested, and did not turn their head back as quickly as they had planned. Important ingredients for cooking dinner can be forgotten, even ones that you were holding in your hand at the store. Do you have a history of losing your keys and/or your wallet? Being lackadaisical about important responsibilities is a side-effect of poor concentration.

Now, a lot of this can be corrected by developing wise habits. We are all creatures of habit, so this approach works. I recommend it for fixing important things like being a better driver and becoming more responsible about not losing things. But that really is a Band-Aid type approach which does nothing to fix the core issue. Wise habits are great, but drilling down into your core and correcting the behavioral issue at a deep level will make your life a lot easier.

People who can focus well are capable of absorbing information in a manner that turns it into knowledge. This means it will be easily accessible for memory recall. Nobody remembers everything, of course. We all have our personal priorities in life. But unless you improve your ability to focus you will have trouble improving yourself in all areas of your life, even hobbies that you are passionate about. Once distraction becomes more normal for you than concentration, you will drift off by habit even when attempting to focus on something that is your heart's greatest desire. This is when it can get ugly, and you find yourself wondering what the heck is wrong with you.

Nothing is actually wrong with you. You have simply allowed a bad habit to take over. Distraction has become the norm for you, instead of concentration. So what we want to do is actually get you back into a habit of concentration in all things, and make that the routine. Unfortunately it may take some work. We will start with the Band-Aid solutions, but work at it until focusing becomes second-nature again. It is a gradual process. But you **can** reprogram yourself in this manner, and the results will be well-worth it.

Getting in Touch with Your Reaction Reflexes

"You are not a chemical – so think before you react."

Humans can lose control of their reaction reflexes quite easily. Reacting without thinking creates a self-destructive condition if our natural reactions are not what we want them to be. From getting mad at someone who doesn't agree with you to responding emotionally over a sarcastic comment, unwanted reactions will define you in an ugly manner to other people. We tend to think we have seen "the real person" when we have seen them react emotionally. Oftentimes an ugly emotional reaction can lead to stress and ultimately, depression.

As an easily distracted person, we are concerned with developing reaction reflexes which result in distraction. This is the source of the bad habit which keeps you from being able to focus. The good news is, you can reprogram your reaction reflexes by consciously getting in touch with them and setting up a determined pro-active mind state. Here are some Tips for accomplishing that.

1) Understand the Difference between Reactive and Pro-active

Let's say a coworker (who you really don't care for) makes a sarcastic comment about your appearance today, which you don't appreciate. Being reactive you may immediately turn on a low confidence, self-conscious, self-criticizing mode and spoil your whole day thinking about how you look and wishing you could somehow get home and change. But a pro-active response might be to just smile at the offender, wish them a good day, and whistle all the way to the coffee pot. You know you look darn good and that whoever was being sarcastic with you was just having a bad day. Now, which of the two reaction reflexes do you think suits your purpose of being focused and happy the whole day? Practice the art of being pro-active by consciously modifying your behavior and see how people start wooing to your good mood!

2) Keep a Check on Yourself

It is quite easy to slip into a negative frame of mind without noticing it until after you have done damage to your reputation. Common culprits include gossip and insecure feelings. Catching this condition early is the trick to not letting it ruin your day. Don't keep running around the office keeping up on the social situations. Get your work done instead. Be yourself, focus on your work, talk only when you cannot avoid it, and you'll find that you're spared from many workplace distractions.

3) Organize Your Disorganized Reflexes

If your workstation looks like a tornado just came through it, this in itself is a distraction trigger. Modify your disorganized way of life and take very conscious steps towards ensuring that everything you do follows a proper routine. Dirty clothes go in the washing machine, keys should be on the table, bills of the current year should be filed and finish off important work first. Procrastinate at any of these and the result is a distracted and disorganized life.

4) Start Keeping a Distraction Log

This can really help with identifying what sort of things cause you to lose focus. Every time you catch yourself drifting, think back to the moment you became distracted and note the thought process and what the trigger seemed to be which sent you off into your own thoughts. Write this information down in a log. You will soon start to notice some common themes. This method really helps you get to understand your own triggers. For example, you might discover that certain topics of conversation trigger a reaction in your mind which causes you to lose focus. This information is invaluable, because it gives you specific locations where you can put up mental roadblocks.

Rerouting Your "Distraction Circuit" into Concentration

Once you have identified the sources of your usual distractions, you can start training your brain to ignore them. Your distraction log (that you compiled in the last chapter) will probably be a great revelation. For example if certain topics of conversation make you lose focus and start thinking on your own, you can become determined to catch yourself very early in that process - thus stopping the mental derailment before it goes very far. After doing this a few times you will start catching it at the very beginning. At that point it will become second-nature to you, and that particular topic of conversation will cease to be a distraction trigger. In fact, you will have trained your brain to turn it into a trigger which makes you concentrate better!

Here are some other tips for rerouting your distraction triggers into focusing triggers.

1) Change Social Network Distraction into Social Network Attention

Facebook, Twitter, G+ are all the major sources of distraction for millions of people around the globe. Since you cannot bring yourself to completely quit all networks, let's change this distraction into something positive. How about you accomplish your task of the day or the week and then proudly state that on the network to receive instant congrats? That would surely be a confidence booster. Therefore as a motivational factor (and as a chance to show off that you're a hard worker) do not put up any status or do not be interactive with anyone until you have accomplished something. Jot down an accomplishment for the day and try achieving that. With the idea of showing off your accomplishment of the day, you can change social network distractions into social network attention. Cool, huh?

2) Change Distractive Socializing into Rewarding Socializing

You don't have to give up on your social life. Instead, you must know how to have a social life that is rewarding as opposed to disturbing. Work your head and bottom off for the week and then when you're certain that you've accomplished something, call up a friend, go out for a pizza, get crazy, come home, smile, relax, and sleep! Now, doesn't that sound enticing? If friends ask you to go out during the week (when you've got loads of work and things to do), reschedule that to a further date until you've completed all your goals. This will keep things balanced and both you and your friends will get to enjoy quality time, without having to worry over the load you have to handle back home.

3) Change from Being Disorganized to Being Organized

Could one of the major sources of distraction in your life be your habit of being disorganized? Have you ever delayed on a task simply because you couldn't get up on time or set up a proper routine? Are you distracted with your recent weight gain simply because you don't want to take out time for a good exercise routine? These are all examples of a person who lacks have a proper routine to follow. The result is that they make a mess of their personal and professional lives. No wonder you cannot concentrate; you are too worried about being able to find things, getting your schedule arranged, getting everything done, and simply organizing your life. It's time you focus on these issues and develop healthy routines.

Free yourself of clutter. Come into a neat and well-organized work station in the morning, come home to a clean and uncluttered home, have a clear schedule in your mind to follow each and every day, and your sources of potential distraction will be greatly reduced.

Changing Your Daydreams into Productive Thinking

We all have been through the childhood experience of sitting in a class and dreaming of Neverland while the teacher goes on and on with their boring lecture. Some of us have allowed that habit to develop to such a degree, however, that we do it in adult life as well, in business meetings or even at the movies. The daydreams are nice. They take us to a place we would rather be. But then, snap! Reality strikes and we realize that we're back where we don't really want to be, and the daydream which was so sweet a moment ago becomes a source of depression.

Some people, however, are not daydreaming about the beach when they get a faraway look on their face during a business meeting. They will snap back into the present with a brilliant idea which pertains to the topic at hand. They have trained themselves to drift off into productive thinking instead of complete distraction. Here are a few tips that can actually help you learn to do that as well.

1) Start Activating Your Conscious Attention

Much of our day can be comprised of simply "going through the motions," or to put it another way, mindlessly performing familiar routines. Time to change that! Start being aware of your surroundings and take notice of your actions, all of the time. The best way to start is by disrupting all familiar daily routines in some specific way, and then purposely remaining in the moment. Try it. Next time you go for coffee intentionally do something like spinning your keys around your figure or singing a silly song. Pay attention to everything around you. Notice what your coworkers are wearing today.

This can start you thinking about all your routine habits. Why do you do a certain thing? What is your objective and how should you react to a certain situation? If you have a habit of daydreaming, make it a point to wake yourself and focus on the environment. Though it's good to take a mental break once in a while, it's a recipe for disaster if your mind keeps wandering away. You will soon become someone who is not alert to his environment and whatever you do will be arduous and half-assed instead of focused and complete.

2) Start Making Realistic Goals

There is no point in dreaming of something that is never going to happen. You are not going to have a new luxury car if you're currently heavily in debt, and you're probably not going to get a call from Hollywood – ever. If you have to dream, if you have to take a thinking break, then think of ways you can enhance your work performance right now, or ways that you can keep your boss happy, ways that you can spend quality time with your family. Dream up solutions to real-time problems. Make real goals and try to implement them. Running away to Neverland is unproductive. You can drift off thinking of ways to improve things instead, which is productive.

3) Change the Course of Your Dreams

If you are like me, you sometimes wish you had a bigger home, a fancier car, and a stronger physique. Perhaps you waste time spending hours dreaming about these possibilities. You can probably achieve these things if you really want to, but will need to stop dreaming and start working towards goals in order to do so.

To have a bigger and better home, you need a better-paying job. How do you get that job? Think of the solution and write it down. Want a toned body? Think of working out in the gym, picture yourself doing that, and write it down. Now isn't that a satisfying way of daydreaming? Even if you snap back to reality, you feel empowered and motivated, rather than deflated. Your daydreams can now become reality with a little determination and focused intelligence.

Daydreaming can be channeled into productive thinking. It will take some effort to do the first few times, but as your familiar routine changes from unproductive dreaming to productive thinking, it will start to become second-nature. Pretty soon you will be the one who comes up with brilliant solutions, gets promotions, and buys a fancy new car.

Learning NOT to Multitask

Multi-tasking is a talent only if you're able to complete all of your work in time without facing deadline issues or quality problems. Otherwise, it is a skill that probably will do more harm than good if you want to improve your concentration skills. Nearly all personal development experts advise people not to multi-task and to focus on one task at a time. This not only helps them to achieve goals, but also to ensure that the results are highly appreciated. Trying to keep too many balls in the air will eventually lead to a declining work quality for most people - and that makes you a failed professional in your field of work.

Disadvantages of Multi-tasking

Short Concentration Span: Your brain becomes actually trained to disengage in the current task to check on other tasks as a habit. This is the opposite of what we want when trying to improve concentration.

Rushing: Your superiors (who you think are yelling at you to meet deadlines) will yell at you even more if the work quality is poor, even when the deadline is met. They do not mean for you to meet the deadline at any cost. If your current workload is too heavy, tell them – and ask them what they want prioritized.

Lack of Dedicated Focus: While working on critical tasks, you need to maintain focus. When you're trying to do 10 things at a time, you're actually scattering all your focus energy and will probably not achieve goals in time for any of them.

Unnecessary Confusion: Trying to juggle a bunch of projects at once will result in at least some confusion. Things that are meant for one project will get mistakenly applied to another. You'll very soon lose track of what you're doing and will have to waste time sorting things out.

Increase in Frustration: Because you are not giving all your attention to one particular task, you will be prone to fall short on all of them, resulting in increased stress levels. Stress is a killer and doesn't help with anything.

How to Avoid Multi-tasking

You need to avoid multitasking in order to perform well on your tasks. Here are some suggestions on how to go about doing that.

Prioritize: You should be able to identify the most important project. Do that now, and **then** start working on the second most important project. If you need help, ask for it.

Do Not Allow Interruptions: When it's your time to work, no one should be interrupting you for any extra favors or companionship. You cannot talk and work at the same time and you surely cannot afford to waste your time. Schedule a specific time for socializing. The rest of the time, don't budge from your work.

Turn-off Chat Programs: Those of us who utilize IM programs are too vulnerable to unscheduled interruptions. We sign in to our PC and within a matter of minutes a friend pops up to discuss something unrelated to the task at hand. Before you know it, you've wasted an hour or so in chatting away uselessly. That is why chatting should not be conducted during work hours; it's not fair for anyone.

Do Not Open Multiple Tabs: This tip is especially for computer users. Do not keep multiple programs and tabs open. Keep only those tabs open of which you need to work on right now. Close web browsers when working on spreadsheets, etc.

Do Not Solve Family Matters at Work: Don't sit and try to solve a family problem at work. Do that tonight. You don't have to make that grocery list right now either. Nor do you have to create and send birthday cards. If you are talking to your significant other on the phone more than twice a day, you are doing it too much. Work time is for work.

Remember, there's a difference between being multitalented and multitasking. Having different skill sets is an asset. Trying to do too many different things at once is a bad habit. Those multitasking are not well-focused on any one task. They will end up regretting the problems which ensue from that.

Five Ways to Conquer the Procrastination Habit

You have an important assignment due on Thursday. On Monday you spend the time chilling out with your friends keeping in mind that you have ample time to work on the assignment. Tuesday you go on with your family for a picnic, knowing you need to somehow start working on the assignment; but you don't care. You wake up late on Wednesday morning and spend the whole day at home resting and watching TV, thinking you'll do it in the evening once you're done with a couple of movies. At night something clicks and suddenly you realize that Thursday morning you have to submit the assignment and you are in a baffled state of mind.

This is what we call procrastination. That is to deliberately avoid doing something just because you don't feel like doing it, or you pretend to be lazy and delay the work which could have been accomplished right away. We are all guilty of it from time to time, but with some people it has become a bad habit. Once a bad habit has manifested itself, it is time to replace it with a good habit. Procrastination is a terrible habit that can literally ruin your life, so it is especially important to weed this one out.

Causes of Procrastination

To overcome a bad habit it is often beneficial to understand where it came from. Some of these reasons you have become a procrastinator may include:

- Stress

- Feeling of being overwhelmed

- Lack of enthusiasm

- Lack of discipline

- Lack of confidence

- Deliberate laziness

- Poor time management

Tips for Conquering your Terrible Procrastination Habit

Let's have a look at some of the ways that may help you to eradicate procrastination:

1) Confession

Always an effective first step. Some people don't realize that they have fallen into this habit and by the time they see it, their life is in a total mess. If you have caught yourself doing this on multiple occasions, it is best to just admit that you are a procrastinator and need to do something about it. Tell yourself "I do not want to be a procrastinator and I will work hard to finish this task today, right now." Repeat these words several times, with as much emotion as you can muster, and then start working on the task. It will probably be completed much faster than you thought possible! Then it will be time for a celebration. Reward yourself. It's like shaking off a heavy burden and giving yourself a chance to relax.

2) Getting to the Origin

For this exercise you need to focus on your feelings, particularly your anxieties. Try to write these sentiments on a piece of paper and then evaluate what you can do to eliminate these problems. Identify the anxiety element in your life and try to see how it connects to your procrastination habit. You'll soon be able to deal with that habit once you see where it really comes from.

3) Time Management

Don't leave things up to tomorrow. Set your goal and try to complete the task in the specified time. There are always several chores that can come up during the course of the day to divert you from your objective. The end result is, time just flies by and you end up having nothing tangible.

4) Start with the Hard Stuff

Try to start the day with what seems like the hardest task. Procrastinators always start with the easiest. This is an unhealthy prioritizing which causes you to have an attitude of always running from anything that sounds difficult. The advantage of picking up the toughest task is that after you have finished it, you will feel relaxed the entire rest of the day and won't be under pressure. Once you have knocked out the tough project, everything else is a piece of cake. Maybe even take a long lunch today!

5) Get Enough Sleep

An adequate amount of sleep at night is very important in order to stay healthy and fit. If your mind and body are both healthy, you can easily meet all the challenges of life and complete all the daily chores in good order. People who think they only need six hours of sleep every night are wrong. You need at least seven.

Procrastination is the leading killer of productivity. Not only does it increase stress and cause you to miss out on stuff, but it hurts your image in the eyes of others. People will think you are not reliable if they see that you procrastinate at little things. Do not let procrastination take a hold on your life. It's understandable to procrastinate once in a blue moon, but if it's happening all the time you need to work on replacing that habit, today.

Arthur Laud

Five Ways to Stop Forgetting Things

Many of us know how it feels to lose something that is important such as your keys, wallet, passport, or airline tickets. You feel like a fool and become very agitated. This is going to happen once in a while no matter how organized you are. However with some people, forgetfulness has become an all-to-frequent occurrence. Once again, this is because a behavioral pattern that was supposed to be temporary has become ingrained in the mind as a bad habit.

Then there are those people who suffer short-term memory lapses, which result in missed appointments and forgotten names. As long as this occurs only occasionally, one can probably regard it as something normal. If this is a frequent occurrence, it should be regarded as a potential medical issue and a doctor should be seen.

Causes of Forgetfulness

• Stress

• Fatigue

• Disorganized

• Unhealthy Diet

• Age Factor (oblivion is a normal phenomenon as we grow older).

Ways to Improve your Brain Power

1) Get organized. Clean the clutter in your life, both physical and mental. Organize your home and your work space for maximum efficiency. Then, organize your schedule and daily routines. An orderly lifestyle lends itself well to strong mental health and clearing your thought processes.

2) Adapt similar practices. Do things in a similar pattern. For example, if you keep your important documents in a particular cabinet then always make the practice of placing them there rather than sometimes in the drawer. Adopting a similar fashion helps create an association between the solution and the problem, and your memory will quit playing games with you.

3) Work out. One of the best ways to boost your brain and mental strength is to exercise. Thirty minutes spent walking or jogging is the best way to get the oxygen flowing into your brain, thereby improving your overall blood circulation and enabling your brain to perform better. Engaging in mental activity such as reading books, solving puzzles or other mind games is also beneficial.

4) Find time for things you love doing. You are a social animal! Being a workaholic is ultimately harmful and will only bring you down. In fact, workaholics are actually less efficient in their work than people who live balanced lives. Get some quality time spent away from a stressful life. Figure out what it is other than your work which keeps you lively and active. Make time for friends and fun. Spend your weekend enjoying a movie, going to a club, visiting your loved ones, playing with your pet, or anything that helps to relax your brain.

5) Eat right. Foods that are rich in omega-3 fatty acids and vitamin B are known to fight depression and memory loss. These include fish, walnuts, cashews, almonds, bananas, pumpkin, apples, whole grains, yogurt, and asparagus. many people take fish oil supplements these days for the sole purpose of improved brain functionality.

Following the above advice will put the odds in your favor when it comes to remembering important things. However the most critical factor is in your own thinking process. You must actually be filing important things in your brain as "important things." If you do that, get proper nutrition, exercise regularly, organize your life and schedule, and create a habit of adapting similar practices, you will probably even be able to find the TV remote when it is jammed under the third couch cushion.

Focusing at Work

Do you love your job? Unfortunately, most people will answer no - that it is just a means to an end for them. But most people work at a job which is at least *tolerable* for them. For a few of us we can say yes, we love what we do.

Whoever we are, wherever we work, most of us still lose focus far too often and find a million excuses to stay distracted. It's hard to maintain concentration at work when there are colleagues bringing you the latest gossip, friends chatting at you on instant messengers, and Facebook to catch up on. The side-effect of all this socializing is a productivity disaster, one that your boss will certainly notice. The longer you let this condition develop, the worse your focusing power will become. Eventually you will turn into a mindless drone who will never get a promotion. Save yourself from those pending self-inflicted disasters by following these tips for focusing better at work.

1) Use Less Technology

Yes. Despite having stickers and ultra-intelligent smartphones, I am recommending that you stick to the traditional mode of note-taking and jotting down ideas on paper. When you actually hold a pen in your hand and note down things in a journal, it sticks in your memory better and has a better chance of you following up on the idea. Wouldn't it be nice to write down daily tasks and tick them off with a red pen every time you're done with one? If you've not tried this yet, you may be surprised at how effective it can be. You'll immediately notice a difference in the approach. Tasks will seem more achievable; more solid and real.

2) Get a Daily Planner

One of the best ways to prioritize tasks and then focus on them is to write down your plans for the next day. Before sleeping, jot down the next day's important projects. The sheer act of writing them down at night helps you to wake up with a proper feel for the day's priorities.

3) Escaping with Headphones

Working in an office environment can make it difficult to avoid coworkers who socialize too much. There is an easy solution to this that nobody will ever blame you for: Headphones! You don't even necessarily have to have music turned on inside of them, nobody will ever know. However you do need to be free from being available by overhead pages and phone calls for this to be practical.

4) Close Instant Messengers

So you think it's harmless to have your IM's on while working? It's actually quite the opposite. People will come online and before you know it, you're going to be discussing the latest movie and delaying your work. Stop chatting, stop checking out Facebook and Twitter. Do that stuff after work, when you're more equipped to dealing with the heartbreaking news of your friend's breakup.

5) Keep Personal Issues At Home

Train your mind to stop taking personal issues to work. By mixing up our personal problems with work, it all looms over us like a dark cloud until we have an aching headache brought on by the double-pressure. If you don't learn to focus on the tasks at hand (instead of continuously mulling over the argument you had with your spouse this morning), you can expect a bad day ahead from every direction.

Similarly, do not bore your coworkers to death with your personal problems. Very few people are your true friend in a corporate world. Your confidential problem will likely end up being just another item on the gossip circuit. Spare yourself from this grief.

When you don't focus at work you end up causing problems not only in your work environment, but ones which carry over into your personal life as well. Which pretty much means that the happiness of your entire life depends on how well you are able to stay focused at work.

Focusing at Play

All work and no play make Jack a dull boy.

We live in a workaholic society. The overwhelming majority of all our time is spent at work, preparing for work, and commuting to and from work. It defines who we really are. The first thing a person you meet is likely to ask you is what you do for a living. This mentality tends to have us thinking work-work-work all the time, even on our days off. It is an unhealthy balance.

On the other hand, there are some people who have learned how to achieve proper balance in their lives. They can detach their mind from work when they leave the office. This is a good way to roll. Focusing on work is important while you are at work, but focusing on play while you are at leisure is equally as important for your overall well-being. You certainly don't want to be drifting off thinking about work when you are at a ball game! Here are some tips to help keep you from doing that.

1) Out for Dinner - Silence all Disturbances

If you're out for dinner, don't spoil it by letting your phone ring nonstop or having email alerts and notifications constantly interrupt. Work hours are over! You have every right to enjoy a peaceful, relaxing dinner with your spouse or friends. We often see people attending phone calls, replying to text messages, and going on and on with their emails even while out at a beautiful restaurant. For crying out loud, shut that phone, engage in the moment and forget the world!

2) Watching a Movie – Stop Thinking About Work

If you've ever left a movie a bit confused because you missed a critical part or two, even though you were sitting there watching the entire time, chances are your mind drifted and you started thinking about work or other things. Maybe something in the movie triggered a distraction circuit. Now you need to see the movie again! This is understandable really, being as movie theatres create a very relaxed atmosphere. Some people even fall asleep at the movies! It's good to relax - but not that much. Try to only see movies which actually seem interesting to you, and be on the alert for your personal distraction triggers during them.

3) Hanging Out – Enjoy the Moment

Let's get this straight. You're going out to have fun and de-stress, not to add further stress. Therefore, do not complain about work to your friends. They are trying to relax as well and don't need the burden. Grow up! Stop complaining and take life a little less seriously. Everyone has workplace issues or personal problems, but nobody really wants to hear about them when they are out to have a little fun. Instead of focusing on yourself, concentrate on enjoying yourself. If you really need someone to talk to, then call them on the phone while you are home and tell them you need to rant a little. That's what friends are for, sure. But it is not the proper time for venting when you get together. Don't call them for a "Let's do something fun" and then end up torturing them with, "I'm so upset over...".

When you play, have fun and be taking a break. Dedicate all that time to that moment. Do not inter-mix work with play. Work is work, play is play - and when you give both of them their deserved time, life begins to take on proper balance.

Arthur Laud

Focusing on Conversations

Have you ever had an embarrassing moment when your boss asked you a question and you went completely blank and then returned a stupid answer, even though you knew the right answer? That state of blankness was probably brought on by a distraction which diverted your focus. A situation like that can make you look foolish if you don't explain your distraction immediately. My own personal issue is a tendency to drift off while my wife is telling me something in her usual less-than-concise manner, which has landed me in the doghouse all too often. I have had to retrain my brain to stay with her whenever she is talking. Here are some tips to keep from drifting during conversations.

1) Learn to Look the Person in the Eye

When talking to a person, keep your head equal to them and look them in the eye. Now that doesn't mean staring at them or being ill mannered. It simply means to not let your gaze wander here and there; not on their nose, on their forehead or on their chin, but in the eye where they can see that you are paying attention. If you have a problem maintaining focus, then this is one great way for you to ensure that the conversation and the person create an impact in your mind. If you haven't noticed, most of the time, we don't focus on people because we let our eyes wander here and there. Stop your eyes from doing that and your mind will start noting down important details.

2) Learn to Train Your Mind to Be Conscious

No one else can control your mind other than you, not even the psychologists or hypnotists you may visit. You and you alone have the ability to control and persuade your mind into doing things the way you want. A great help towards maintaining your attention in conversations is to train your mind to be alert, aware, and conscious. Stop it from assuming and from thinking irrelevant things. Take a genuine interest in the person, talk to them, and respond without trying to help them complete their sentences (people hate that, and man is it embarrassing when you get it wrong). Train your mind to listen to the other person and very soon you will be able to give spontaneous replies without losing focus.

3) Learn to be Slow but Confident

You're not catching a train and you are certainly not obliged to answer anyone word for word. So stop worrying about what people say and how you will respond. Conversations should develop naturally and not be arduous. Be slow with your words when you reply. Take your time and speak confidently. This is extremely important for interviews or high level meetings where you need to put in all your focus and reply in a confident tone. Do not be in a hurry to reply and you will seldom stumble over your words. Most importantly, be honest. If you don't understand a point, make sure you let the person know. People can tell when you are faking it, just to try and look better. They will respect you more if you ask for clarification once in a while. When we are honest with ourselves as well as with others, and forego the urge to look smart, we don't get distracted as much.

Arthur Laud

Meeting Deadlines

We are all guilty of occasionally missing deadlines. Meeting tight deadlines can be one of the most infuriating tasks, even for people that have super-human powers of concentration. Deadlines create pressure. Pressure can result in stress. It's like you have a sword looming over your head at times. Even so, many people would seemingly rather be cut by the sword than learn to escape it. Yes, sheer procrastination and laziness are leading causes of missing deadlines and even though we know the negative effects of this habit, we still don't care. It's crazy. If you develop a habit of missing deadlines, you risk your professional career. That is how detrimental bad habits can be to your life. Here are a few tips for you to help you deal with meeting deadlines effectively.

1) Understand Your Potential and Work Capacity

In order to meet deadlines, you have to first understand your potential, your skill level, and your work capacity. How fast are you and how efficiently can you perform a task without affecting quality? What is your capacity for staying focused and do you have a lot of distractions in your environment? These are critical considerations which should be addressed **before** accepting a project. If you find out that a task is much more involved than you originally thought, negotiate a deadline extension sooner rather than later. Either way, never take up a task without having a clear understanding of what you are actually capable of performing.

2) Never Promise More Than You Can Deliver

Due to miscalculations or overconfidence, at times we promise more than we can deliver simply because we don't comprehend the reality of the situation at hand. This is especially true for freelancers who take on multiple projects and end up delaying the deadlines for all of them. So unless you have supersonic speed with excellent quality control, be very careful about accepting multiple projects. Not only will this make you seem as a fool, but also as someone incredibly unreliable. Review the previous chapter about multi-tasking if you are still having trouble in this area.

3) Create a Realistic Routine and Stick to It

Easier said than done perhaps, but having healthy daily routines allow you to accomplish more. Set a specific time period for each task, keeping in mind other important activities. You don't have to work day and night or overtime for a task if you know how to create a well-balanced routine. Many of us fail simply because we lack the serious dedication of getting properly organized.

4) Talk to Family and Friends about Your Need for Space

Explain your work routine to everyone in your personal life and ask for their support. Hopefully, they will get the hint not to disturb you when you're working, and understand that you need a certain amount of space and freedom to do your work undisturbed. This will make your cell phone beep at you less. When you take your family into confidence over your work schedule, they will usually respect this condition and make sure that you are not disturbed. The same goes for colleagues. There's always a break time to catch up on conversations. During stringent work hours, nobody should be distracting you. If you don't get distracted, you can focus well and perform better in your work.

5) Take it One Day at a Time

For large projects, break it up into parts and try to accomplish the tasks according to the time set. Take it one day at a time and you'll find yourself quite relaxed as the deadline approaches. There will be no hurrying around and less tension.

Employees who understand the value of deadlines and take them seriously are always appreciated by their managers or clients.

Five Fun Games that Help Develop Powers of Concentration

Whoever said you need to get all serious-like in order to learn to focus better? You can do it the fun way - a way which also enriches your mind. There are great games that will enhance your concentration powers and thinking abilities. If you are unfamiliar with them, or have never been any good at them, it might be frustrating in the beginning. Pick up a strategy guide for a couple of these games! You will probably learn to love them and at the same time be put on a path to achieving strong mental powers.

1) Chess

The ultimate mind-strategy game. Chess is a game of complete information and requires heavy concentration to play well. It's like learning the art of war. For that you have to use all your brain power to come up with dynamic methods. Get a book that teaches you the openings. Open a free account at

Chess.com if you can't find an opponent in your home. Start by playing other novices and learn the openings. This wonderful game will work wonders on your mind and your ability to stay focused.

2) Crossword Puzzles

Crosswords are a great way to test your vocabulary as well as your logical powers. Since crossword clues usually involve terms that you encounter in everyday life, they also test your memory and force you to think. These word puzzles are not only good in building a strong vocabulary, but they also increase your knowledge and short-term memory recall.

3) Jigsaw Puzzles

Ever completed a 5,000 piece jigsaw puzzle? They are superb for relieving stress as well as being a good exercise for your mind. The smaller the puzzle pieces, the more fun! You may have to sit for days to be able to complete a whole picture. During that time, you might be surprised to discover that you have found solutions to your personal problems while working on the puzzle. There is just something about jigsaw puzzles that relaxes your brain to a point where it can find workable solutions to problems you are facing in other areas of your life. Some top executives have held this secret for many years. Beware though, jigsaw puzzles are addictive and you will be tempted to stay up too late working on them. Better than watching reality TV though, that's for sure.

4) Riddles

Riddles are a centuries-old pastime used for sharpening the mind and engaging in a battle of wits. There is even a riddle puzzle in the Bible (Sampson's riddle). However, it has become something of a lost art. Today, most of us would have to struggle to come up with the right answer to the coded sentence structure of riddles. People in earlier times actually used riddles to convey secret messages or talk about sensitive issues in the country. If you learn the art of coding and decoding riddles, you will certainly enhance your critical and analytical thinking power. I recommend getting a basic book on the lost art of riddles.

5) Tongue Twisters

Yes, really. Many people hate them. However they are quite a beneficial exercise. Tongue twisters will increase your verbal capacity while forcing you to memorize and repeat words in a swift momentum. Try saying this without stammering, "She sells seashells on the seashore." Say it until you perfect it and you may start laughing at the difficulty it first presented. It feels pretty good when you master one however, and makes a pretty good trick to show off at happy hour.

There are many other logical games that you can play to enhance your mental powers. With today's smartphones and tablets, it's even easier to get your hands on such games. Whenever you have spare time, boost your mind with these mental exercises and you will be surprised at how alert and active your mind will become.

Conclusion

Many of us go through life without giving a second thought on how many thousands of hours we have wasted on unproductive daydreams and distractions. It isn't really a problem for a lot of people who only use it as a temporary reprieve from realty; in fact for them, it is a healthy diversion. They are people who are blessed with a natural ability to stay focused on demand. For the rest of us, becoming distracted has started to become an undesirable element in our lives, and can even develop into a chronic problem. Being easily distracted and procrastinating on important tasks can eventually disrupt your entire life if you don't take control of it.

This short book was written to help those people who find it difficult to concentrate on daily tasks. A condition of constantly losing focus and being unable to concentrate cannot normally be cured by drugs, herbal supplements, or psychologist bills because ultimately it is up to you to decide what you want your mind to accomplish. Either let it waste away or take a stand against this snowballing problem. It is not terribly difficult to do, but will require a little work and determination to see it through. Start correcting the unwanted behavior today. Follow the advice given about gradually reprogramming bad habits which have become unwanted reaction reflexes in your brain, and you will soon overcome your focusing issues. It's up to you.

Books by Arthur Laud

How to Ask for a Raise After Taking a 2-Hour Lunch: *Arm yourself with perfect preparation, timing, approach, and presentation when asking for that raise!*

The Balance Beam for Workaholics: *How to calm down, smell the roses, not have a heart attack, enjoy life, and actually improve your productivity as a result*

Midlife Career-Change Tips for Burnouts: *How to start over from scratch, get pumped again, and wind up in a good financial position*

Confidence Building for Mice: *How to Raise your Self Esteem and Conquer the World... even if you are a bit on the timid side.*

Hocus Pocus, you're Focused! *A Daydreamer's Guide to Developing Powers of Concentration*

Goal-Setting for Slugs: *How to get what you want from life, even if you are a little slow out the gate.*

Minimalizing for Material Girls: *How to do this super cool trendy minimalizing thing and still keep all your great stuff*

Tame your Tornado: *How to Organize Every Aspect of your Life for Success and Happiness.*

Public Speaking for Frankenstein: *Learn how to overcome stage fright, build trust, entertain, persuade, and have fun speaking even if you are less than eloquent*

Relationship Advice for Prima Donnas: *How to Have Healthy Functional Relationships with Family, Friends, and Co-Workers... even if you are a tad on the selfish side.*

www.ingramcontent.com/pod-product-compliance
Lightning Source LLC
Chambersburg PA
CBHW071121240526
45465CB00022B/738